Markus Persson

NOTCH

Creator of MINECRAFT

Tamra Orr

PURPLE TOAD
PUBLISHING

PURPLE TOAD
PUBLISHING

Printing   1   2   3   4   5   6   7   8   9

A Beacon Biography

Big Time Rush
Carly Rae Jepsen
Drake
Harry Styles of One Direction
Jennifer Lawrence
Kevin Durant
Lorde
Markus "Notch" Persson, Creator of *Minecraft*
Neil deGrasse Tyson
Peyton Manning
Robert Griffin III (RG3)

Publisher's Cataloging-in-Publication Data
Orr, Tamra.
   Markus "Notch" Persson, Creator of Minecraft / written by Tamra Orr.
     p. cm.
             Includes bibliographic references.
             ISBN 9781624691201
             1. Persson, Markus, 1979–Juvenile literature.2. Minecraft (Game). 3. Computer programmers—Biography. 4. Computer games—Programming—Juvenile literature. 5. Computer games—Design. I. Series : Beacon Biographies Collection Two.
   GV1463 2015
   794.8

Library of Congress Control Number: 2014912093

eBook ISBN: 9781624691218

ABOUT THE AUTHOR: Tamra Orr is a full-time author living in the Pacific Northwest with her husband, children, cat, and dog. She graduated from Ball State University in Muncie, Indiana. She has written more than 300 books about many subjects, ranging from historical events and career choices to controversial issues and biographies. On those rare occasions that she is not writing a book, she is reading one.

PUBLISHER'S NOTE: The data in this book has been researched in depth, and to the best of our knowledge is factual. Although every measure is taken to give an accurate account, Purple Toad Publishing makes no warranty of the accuracy of the information and is not liable for damages caused by inaccuracies. This story has not been authorized or endorsed by Markus Persson.

CONTENTS

Markus Persson had no idea that incredible success was just around the corner.

Breaking
a Record

Mornings had changed recently for Markus "Notch" Persson. In fact, almost everything had changed since his release of *Minecraft* in 2010.

On this summer morning, he did what he had started to do every morning in recent months. He sat down to check his email. Every time someone bought a copy of his game, he would get an email notification. Many of the people buying *Minecraft* lived in the United States, so the emails would come in while he was sleeping at his home in Sweden. Seeing those sales helped put this young game designer in a good mood for the rest of the day.

When he saw the number of emails he had, Notch thought there had to be a mistake. There were more than 400![1] This was definitely a new record, but in coming months, that record would be broken again and again.

Unlike other computer and video games, *Minecraft* was not available on the big-time outlets. Gamers could not find it on Steam. It was not on Xbox Arcade. Instead, gamers had to go directly to Minecraft.net. They had to register, put in their credit card details, and then wait for the game to download. Who was willing to do this in a day and age when other sites made the process so much faster and easier?

Apparently thousands of players were eager to do so. By the end of summer 2010, more than 20,000 people around the world had purchased *Minecraft*. A page on *Minecraft's* site lists the number of players who have bought just the PC/Mac version of the game. The number is staggering! Notch would never have been able to keep up with all of his daily emails.

Since 2010, *Minecraft* has done nothing but grow. By late February 2014, 14.3 million people had bought the PC/Mac version of the game.[2] By July, that number had climbed to nearly 16 million—and that did not include sales for Xbox, PlayStation, or other console versions. In fact, a *Minecraft* data analyst reported in June 2014, "Minecraft console editions together just passed Minecraft for PC/Mac. And across all platforms, we've sold almost 54 million copies."[3]

Minecraft has captured the adoration of gamers, as well as growing attention from educators, politicians, architects, city planners, and other professionals. In this sandbox game, players can roam freely. To play, gamers collect blocks of natural resources and use them to create anything they want, from barns and houses to skyscrapers and underground lairs; airplanes and other

Raising pigs on a farm in *Minecraft*

The Les Cayes waterfront in Haiti, recreated in *Minecraft*.

*Pontus Westerberg speaks about how **Minecraft** is used by UN Habitat and their Block by Block program (inset). When **Minecraft** was given to Haiti fishermen unable to read, they were able to redesign one of their waterfronts. In the past, it had been plagued by flooding, and the new design added a protective sea wall. Architects built the fishermen's design and it was successful.*

transportation devices; furniture; and even people to populate a new house, town, city, or world. Players must farm or gather food for themselves, and in some modes, they must find a safe place to sleep, lest they be gobbled up by monsters like spiders, zombies, and the exploding green *Creepers.*

The game is used by hundreds of thousands of students in classrooms across the planet, as well as for designing urban spaces for the United Nations Human Settlements Program. It has inspired Minecon, a yearly conference that attracts fans and players from all over the world. In 2010, Minecon started with 50 people showing up in Bellevue, Washington. By 2013, thousands attended in Orlando, Florida. When tickets went on sale online, 2,500 were sold in *three seconds!*

Notch grew up 3 hours north of Stockholm, Sweden, where he was born. His mother was a nurse while his father worked for the railroad.

Discovering
Computer Code

Markus Persson was born on June 1, 1979. He grew up near the city of Edsbyn, near Sweden's east coast. His father, Birger, was a railroad worker. He left the family while the children were in their teens. His mother, Rita, continued to raise Markus and his sister, Anna, alone. Years later, Persson remembered a special time with his dad when he was very young. He told *The New Yorker,* "My strongest early memory is of my dad dragging me through very deep snow on a sled. I looked up at him and he seemed annoyed at me. Perhaps it was tough work, dragging me, or perhaps I had been crying. And I realized that—hang on—he's actually a real person, with his own perception of things. It's not just me looking at things; he is also looking at things."[1]

Before Birger left, however, he brought home something that sparked his son's imagination: a Commodore 128, a large, clunky computer by today's standards. Produced from 1985 through 1989, it featured a black monitor lit by green letters. In addition to the computer, the family began subscribing to a computer magazine.

The Commodore 128

"It was a huge [magazine], newspaper format, and it had program listings in it that you could enter into your computer to get a silly little game or fun effect and things like that," Notch explained in an interview with Alex Handy. "I started entering them, and noticed that they broke or did different things if you changed what you entered. I don't remember exactly how fast this process was, but I know I made my first own program when I was eight years old. It was an extremely basic text adventure game when you had to enter the correct sentences to move on to the next room ('open the door,' 'kill the ninja,' that stuff)."[2]

Anna was his helper during those days. "My sister would read the lines out to me and I would tap them into the computer," Notch told *The New Yorker*. "After a while, I figured out that if you didn't type out exactly what they told you then something different would happen, when you finally ran the game. That sense of power was intoxicating."[3]

Like many other kids in the 1980s, Notch was fascinated with these games. It wasn't long before he got the next model of computer, the C64. While he does not remember the first game he ever played on it, he remembers the first game he ever bought: *The Bard's Tale.* "I didn't understand anything of it, but I remember it feeling very magical and wonderful," he told Handy. "One of my earliest gaming memories is playing *Raid on Bungling Bay* on a black-and-white TV in our living room. I'd mostly fly

The Bard's Tale

Bungling Bay. *In this part of the game, Notch would fight to control the helicopter before it was shot down.*

around for a bit then try to land on the carrier again before the scary jet fighters started appearing."[4]

The first time he designed his own game, he was nine. "It was purely mechanical in the beginning," he admitted in an interview for BAFTA, the British Academy of Film and Television Arts. "I was just curious about how it worked and what the weird commands actually meant. The first thing I wrote . . . was a text adventure. You had to input the exact right text or otherwise you would fail. The story was kind of random. There were four or five different rooms and one of them had a typical spaghetti western theme. I used ASCII characters as the graphics."[5] *ASCII* (ask-ee) is a computer program that uses numbers to represent letters and characters in order to create graphics.

What Notch was able to accomplish on his own was amazing. He had not had any special classes or training. He has said, "I would consider myself 100% self-taught. I don't have any advanced education at all."[6]

Those beginning days of learning computer code gave Persson a focus during his parents' divorce and his father's use of drugs and alcohol. It also fed a curiosity that would point his life in a new—and incredibly successful—direction. His dream of becoming a police officer was pushed aside. Computer programming was his new passion!

Markus used his passion for computer programming to create something completely new.

Persson knew by the age of fifteen that he wanted to spend his time programming and playing computer games, but he did not know how that fascination could lead to a job.

As a teenager in school, Persson was not necessarily popular. He did not like sports. He did not have any girlfriends. He did not even get perfect grades. He found his niche, however, with a group of other teen programmers. They would get together to see who could design the best program on their Atari ST computers. "One time, I managed to fill the screen with huge text that scrolled incredibly quickly," he recalled in an interview with *The New Yorker*. "My friend was on vacation, so I put the code on a disc and attached a Post-it note, saying, 'Look what I did!' and left it in his mailbox."[1] He took the nickname "Notch" because, as he told Craig Ferguson on a TV talk show, all computer nerds need nicknames. Did the word have special meaning for him? No, he just liked it!

Although the use of home computers was growing quickly in the 1990s, classes about how to make games were still in development. Persson's teachers wanted to foster his interest, but they were not sure how to direct him. A number suggested he study graphic design as a starting point, so he did. His first job was as a Web designer. He loved it, and learned a great deal, but it did not make him as happy as he had hoped. "I didn't stay there, because I was a bit arrogant and thought I could just go and make games," he says. "But then the dot-com crash happened and I couldn't get a job."[2]

Living at home with his mother was the next step, and it was frustrating. Although he finally found a job as a programmer and designer for Game Federation, and then King.com, Notch still was not happy. During the day, he created games as fast as he possibly could. At night, he would develop his own creative games and then enter them in competitions. Although he learned an amazing amount at work about design, he hardly had time to absorb and understand it. "The most limiting factor was that we were making [the games] so fast," he told BAFTA. "It was kind of intense. We spent one or two months on each game. During my time at

Persson has inspired many young people to start studying programming.

King.com I made around 20 to 30 games. I was the programmer and I had a games designer and an artist. That was basically it. The thing I learned there was how to actually finish projects, which was very, very valuable."[3] Notch was at King.com for four and a half years. While he was there, he helped create popular games such as *Funny Farm, Luxor,* and *Carnival Shootout.* "I was learning things about game design in my day job," he recalls in *The New Yorker* interview, "but really it was the puzzle-solving nature of programming that appealed."[4]

Although Birger had been separated from his family for years, he kept in touch with his son and sometimes offered feedback on Notch's games. "He usually gave me the fatherly version of game criticism, saying, 'They're brilliant, of course,'" Notch told *The New Yorker.* When he finally made the decision to cut back on his job so he could spend more time at home working on his own games, his father encouraged him. "He was the only person who supported my decision," Notch said. "He was proud of me and made sure I knew. When I added the monsters to *Minecraft,* he told me that the dark caves became too scary for him. But I think that was the only true criticism I ever heard from him."[5]

Over the next few years, Notch grew closer to his father. When he lost him in 2011 to suicide, it was a terrible time for him. In a blog post a year after his father's death, Notch wrote, "I now have an entire life to live without him existing."[6]

After being part-time for months, Notch quit his job completely on his thirty-first birthday. This would give him all the time he needed to finish the game he had been working on since 2009—a world made of blocks that he called *Minecraft.*

Minecraft *players can create mighty fortresses, and then work to defend them.*

Building Block by Block

At first glance, many people wonder why *Minecraft* is so incredibly popular across the globe. Does it have impressive special effects? Not really. Realistically designed characters and scenes? Not even close. Quests and multiple levels to achieve? Nope. Terrific benefits when you win? There's no winning or losing in the game. Detailed instructions on how to play? Once again—no. It's all up to you, the player, to figure it out.

So why do so many people love this game?

Minecraft is limited by nothing but the player's imagination. You can play alone, with a partner, with a team, or with a group. In creative mode, you can build, play, and fly endlessly in a 3-D world. You can build up and tear down. You can change colors or shift shapes. You can do something as simple as chop down a tree and then use the wood to make a house. You can also work with others to create an entire *Star Wars, Harry Potter,* or *Lord of the Rings* universe. If you go into survival mode, you can battle creepers, skeletons, and zombie pig men. You can solve problems and figure out challenges. The *Minecraft* site explains it this way: "It [the game] can be about adventuring with friends or watching the sun rise over a blocky ocean. Brave players battle terrible

MAKING MINECRAFT

Dwarf Fortress

Dungeon Keeper

Infiniminer

Markus Persson had long wanted to create a word building game, complete with role playing elements found in RPG games. He was influenced by games like Dwarf Fortress, Dungeon Keeper, and Roller Coaster Tycoon. Of all the games, it was Infiniminer that inspired Persson the most. Infiniminer had players building structures and digging for minerals in a sandbox world. It was just the type of game Persson had been wanting to create.

Thanks in part to Infiniminer, Markus learned how to create a 3-D environment done completely in low-res textures. The game showed him a way he could render Minecraft's vast landscapes and art. In about one week, he had written the basic version of Minecraft right in his apartment in Stockholm.

Soon he was joining Mensa, the largest and oldest high IQ society in the world, and being chosen by Time magazine as one of the top 100 most influential people in the world in 2013.

things in The Nether. Or you can visit a land of mushrooms if it sounds more like your cup of tea."[1]

Ask players why they love the game so much, and they will give these answers and many more. Ask Notch? He admits that the popularity of the game has been absolutely shocking—and something he never thought would happen. "I expected it to be about six to twelve months of work, and hoped that it might earn enough money to fund development of a subsequent game," he told *The New Yorker.*[2]

Notch is a strong believer in little companies. He created his own company in 2009 to produce *Minecraft,* naming it Mojang, which is Swedish for "gadget." Even with the explosive growth of the game, by 2014, the company had only about 35 employees. When *Minecraft* started selling thousands and thousands of copies, big companies like Valve tried to hire Notch. He turned them down, telling journalist John Walker, "I don't want to work for Valve. I want to be Valve."[3]

As more and more people buy and download *Minecraft,* Notch makes more money. He had never been rich before and found it a little confusing. "The money is a strange one," he said. "I'm slowly getting used to it, but it's a Swedish trait that we're not supposed to be proud of what we've done. We're supposed to be modest. So at first,

The Mojang offices are here, where every Friday, Notch gives his staff a free day to play videogames.

Not only is Notch's game a bestseller, but so is the merchandise associated with it, including action figures, paper build sets, toy torches, posters, and hats like this one and its "creeper" face.

I had a really hard time spending any of the profits. Also, what if the game stopped selling? But after a while, I thought about all of the things I'd wanted to do before I had money. So I introduced a rule: I'm allowed to spend half of anything I make. That way I will never be broke. Even if I spend extravagant amounts of money, I will still have extravagant amounts of money."[4] Notch also shares a huge percentage of the profit from the game with all of his employees. In 2012, he distributed $3 million among all of his "Mojangstas," as he calls them.[5]

Notch enjoys watching what people do with the game he created. He often reads about the modifications or "mods" people have made to the game, which allows them to create huge worlds modeled after books and movies. He also enjoys seeing what tricks they have learned and sometimes tries to do them too. "I like to dig out caves," he told Walker. "I see a hole through to another cave and I have to continue on, clear every passage." He admits he can't do the corner jump he sees some players do, and says with a laugh, "But it's MY game!"[6]

Notch began working on several other games. One was called *0x10c*—a name that he calls "a riddle."[7] It is a trading game set in space. It was slow going. He admits it has been terribly hard to follow up such a huge hit as *Minecraft*. "I definitely think Minecraft is a freak thing," he said to *The New Yorker*. He fears there was no way to repeat the success it brought him. "With *Minecraft* it was just easier," he admitted, "because nobody knew who I was. Now I post a new idea, and millions of people scrutinize it. There's a conflict between the joy of being able to do whatever I want, and the remarkable pressure of a watching world. I don't know how to switch it off."[8]

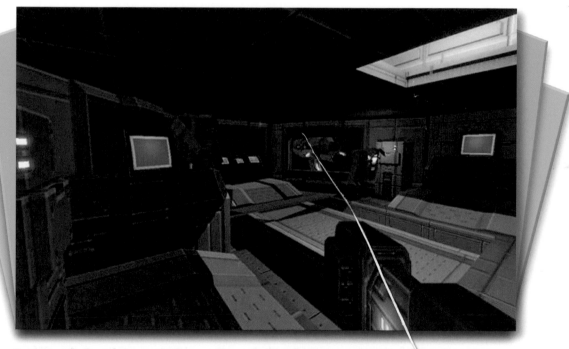

0x10[c] *was based partially on the science fiction series* Firefly. *In it, players could pilot spaceships, land on planets, or try to capture alien creatures. Many gamers still hope this game will be developed.*

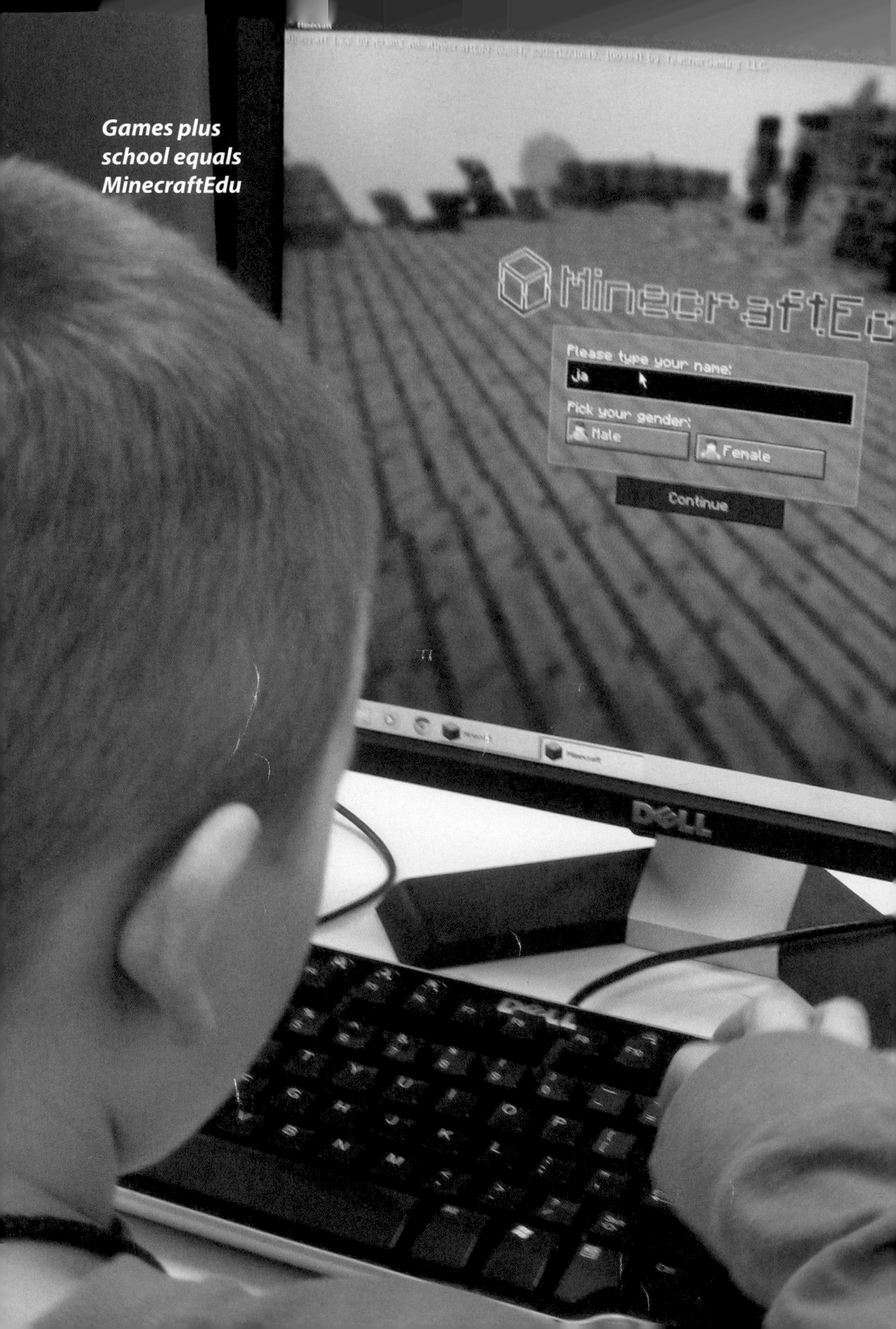

Games plus school equals MinecraftEdu

Millions of copies of *Minecraft* have been downloaded all over the world. The game is played on desktops, laptops, smart phones, and game consoles, so players can take it almost anywhere.

Teachers have even brought a game into classrooms. In early 2013, a school in Stockholm, Sweden, required its students play *Minecraft*. Monica Ekman, a teacher at the school, explained to *The New York Times*, "They [students] learn about city planning, environmental issues, getting things done, and even how to plan for the future."[1] Many other schools are finding ways to use the game too. A group called MinecraftEdu is making sure that is possible. Their goal is to get *Minecraft* into classrooms throughout the world. Through MinecraftEdu, schools can buy the game for less, plus teachers are offered custom programs for their students. Special training shows teachers the many different ways to put *Minecraft* to use in language arts, history, geography, and other classes. Joel Levin, who runs the site, says that this game is being used to teach kids about everything from science to city planning to speaking a new language.[2]

Minecraft is a huge success—but what is next for its inventor? Notch is not sure, but he sure does have a bunch of ideas! "I have many games in mind. . . . I have this weird town simulation thing, which is basically a single-character *Sims,*" he said to John Walker, referring to the *Sims* video game series in which players can create characters that eat, sleep, and go to work. "You're just one character in the town, just living. The setting would be a real city, but it would have the same approach as *Minecraft,*" he continued. "If it's fun, it gets added. So it wouldn't be a super-realistic city simulator. It would be my take on what real life is. I like the idea of calm. I like focusing on what's actually fun. *Sims,* well, it is kind of fun when you get used to it, lots of it is doing the same thing over and over a lot. I want something which is . . . something more playful." Another idea he had was for a football game, only with fantasy creatures instead of the usual players. "If you have a troll and a goblin on the same team, the troll might eat the goblin. Stuff like that," he added.[3]

In December 2011, Notch stepped down as lead developer for *Minecraft*—although he is still the owner of Mojang. Another *Minecraft* programmer, Jens "Jeb" Bergensten, became the new lead developer.[4] Besides the regular *Minecraft* game, Bergensten was also heading up development of *Minecraft*—*Pocket Edition.*

Minecraft—Pocket Edition

Wearing creeper shirts are Notch (standing on left) and Jeb Bergensten (standing on right). Bergensten is now lead programmer for **Minecraft**, *adding horses, rabbits, and making the world even bigger.*

Notch plans to continue keeping his *Minecraft* fans happy, creating new games, and juggling—and sharing—his profits. He posted online to *Reddit* that he has plans on how to handle the money *Minecraft* has earned him. "I think the right way to use money like this is to set a decent portion aside to make sure my family is comfortable, spend some on living out your dreams, and then try to put the rest towards making society a better place," he wrote. "For me, this includes charities that help children, and

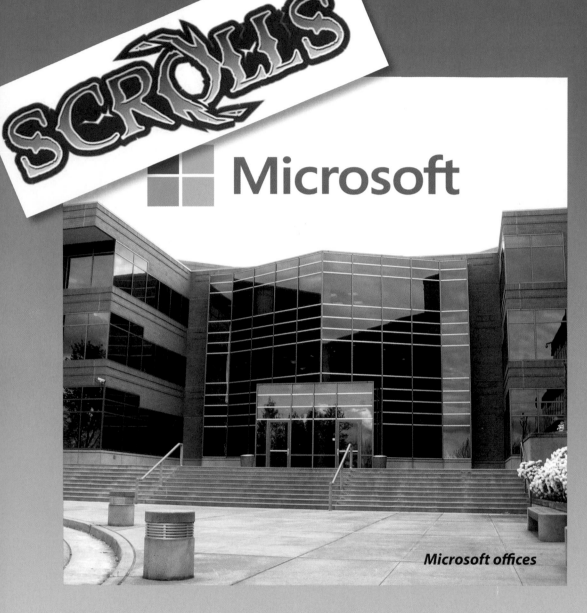

Microsoft offices

Notch had another success in the online fantasy card game **Scrolls**. After the success of **The Lego Movie**, *plans are underway for a big screen version of* **Minecraft** *with* **The Lego Movie** *producer Roy Lee developing it for Warner Brothers.*

Despite these projects, Notch was ready to move on. On September 15, 2014, he sold Mojang to Microsoft for a staggering $2.5 billion. A few weeks later, in November 2014, he walked out of the building for the last time.

Who knows where the road will lead for Markus Persson? For now, he is enjoying his new driver's license, playing fun video games he loves like **Legend of Grimrock II,** *and thinking about what kind of programming he wants to do next.*

charities that help promote freedoms I think are vital in the coming dozens of years.[5]

Of course, Notch has some important advice for young people who hope to create games like he did. "If you're trying to do something successful and unique, the only advice that really matters is not to listen to advice (including this advice!)," he told journalist Will Freeman. "You will try to define yourself in terms of what other people have done and so you will never do something that is original."[6]

Clearly, if there is one thing that Notch knows, it is how to be original. The originality of *Minecraft* changed people's minds about what games can do. It reminds people of all ages, all over the world, how important it is to create, build, and imagine—even if it is one block at a time.

1972	Nolan Bushnell and Ted Dabney start Atari Inc.; their game *Pong* is a quick success.
1979	Markus "Notch" Persson is born on June 1, to Rita and Birger Persson, in Sweden.
1980s	Birger Persson brings home a Commodore 128.
1985	*The Bard's Tale* computer role playing game is released.
1986	Persson creates his first computer game at age 7.
1990	Birger, battling drug and alcohol addiction, leaves the family.
1994	Notch gets his first job as a Web designer.
1996	He begins working as a programmer and game designer for Flash games.
1997	*Dungeon Keeper* computer game is released for PC.
2003	Persson co-develops *Wurm Online*, a massively multiplayer online role playing game.
2006	*Dwarf Fortress* is released.
2009	*Infiniminer* is released. Notch begins writing code for *Minecraft;* he creates Mojang, the company that will produce it.
2010	*Minecraft* is released.
2011	Notch's father commits suicide. In December, Notch steps down as lead developer of *Minecraft,* but he continues to run the business.
2012	Notch works on his space game 0x10^c, whose name he calls "a riddle"; he soon abandons the project.
2013	Persson halts development of 0x10$^{c.}$
2014	By June, *Minecraft* has sold over 54 million copies. A *Minecraft* movie is in the works. Notch sells Mojang to Microsoft for 2.5 billion dollars. He leaves the company.

FURTHER READING

Works Consulted

Bilton, Nick. "Disruptions: *Minecraft,* an Obsession and an Educational Tool." *The New York Times: Bits.* September 15, 2013. http://bits.blogs.nytimes.com/2013/09/15/minecraft-an-obsession-and-an-educational-tool/?_php=true&_type=blogs&_r=0

Carless, Simon. "Interview: Markus Persson on Bringing Achievements to Minecraft." *Game. Set. Watch.* February 28, 2011. http://www.gamesetwatch.com/2011/02/interview_markus_persson_on_br.php

Childs, Sophie. "The Benefit of Minecraft for Children." *Yahoo! News UK and Ireland.* November 18, 2013. http://uk.news.yahoo.com/benefits-minecraft-children-160600445.html#EUh2ACD

Freeman, Will. "Interview: The Minecraft Man." *Develop.* October 28, 2010. http://www.develop-online.net/interview/interview-the-minecraft-man/0116892

Handy, Alex. "Interview: Markus 'Notch' Persson Talks Making Minecraft." *Gamasutra.* March 23, 2010. http://www.gamasutra.com/view/news/27719/Interview_Markus_Notch_Persson_Talks_Making_Minecraft.php

Hilliard, Kyle. "Minecraft's Markus 'Notch' Persson Talks about His Millionaire Status." *Game Informer.* February 2, 2013. http://www.gameinformer.com/b/news/archive/2013/02/02/minecraft-39-s-notch-talks-about-his-millionaire-status.aspx

Johnson, Eric. "Book Excerpt: How *Minecraft* Creator Markus Persson Almost Took a Job at Valve." *All Things D.* December 9, 2013. http://allthingsd.com/20131209/book-excerpt-how-minecraft-creator-markus-persson-almost-took-a-job-at-valve/

Kolakowski, Nick. "*Minecraft:* Small Story of a Big Game." *Slashdot.* October 21, 2013. http://slashdot.org/topic/cloud/minecraft-small-story-of-a-big-game/

Kolman, Rachel. "*Minecraft* Can Now Be Played in School." *WebProNews.* November 17, 2013. http://www.webpronews.com/minecraft-can-now-be-played-in-school-2013-11

Lemon, Marshall. "*Minecraft* Becomes a United Nations Development Tool." *The Escapist.* September 6, 2012. http://www.escapistmagazine.com/news/view/119457-Minecraft-Becomes-a-United-Nations-Development-Tool

Machell, Ben. "How Minecraft Creator Markus Persson Built the World." *The Weekend Australian Magazine.* December 7, 2013. http://www.theaustralian.com.au/news/features/how-minecraft-creator-markus-persson-built-the-world/story-e6frg8h6-1226776074148

"Markus 'Notch' Persson, Mojang CEO, Gives $3 Million to Employees." *Huffington Post.* March 2, 2012. http://www.huffingtonpost.com/2012/03/02/markus-notch-persson-gives-3-million_n_1317396.html

McVeigh, Tracy. "*Minecraft:* How a Game with No Rules Changed the Rules of the Game Forever." *The Guardian.* November 16, 2013. http://www.theguardian.com/technology/2013/nov/16/minecraft-game-no-rules-changed-gaming

Minecraft, Statistics. February 23, 2014. https://minecraft.net/stats

O'Brien, Chris. "A Virtual Way to Be with Their Deported Friend." *LA Times.* September 2, 2013. http://www.latimes.com/local/la-fi-c1-rodrigos-world-20130902-dto,0,2239765.htmlstory

Parkin, Simon. "The Creator." *The New Yorker.* April 5, 2013. http://www.newyorker.com/online/blogs/elements/2013/04/the-minecraft-creator-markus-persson-faces-life-after-fame.html

Persson, Markus. *The Word of Notch.* http://notch.tumblr.com/

Roberts, Paul. "An Interview with Minecraft Creator Markus 'Notch' Persson." *Den of Geek.* December 16, 2010. http://www.denofgeek.us/games/12092/an-interview-with-minecraft-creator-markus-%E2%80%98notch%E2%80%99-persson

Russell, Jamie. "Markus Persson: Interview." *BAFTA Guru.* March 14, 2012. http://guru.bafta.org/markus-persson-interview

Statt, Nick. "Markus 'Notch' Persson: The Mind Behind *Minecraft* (Q&A)." *CNet.* November 7, 2013. http://news.cnet.com/8301-1023_3-57611112-93/markus-notch-persson-the-mind-behind-minecraft-q-a/

Walker, John. "A Day in the Life of Minecraft Creator Mojang." *Rock, Paper, Shotgun.* March 7, 2011. http://www.rockpapershotgun.com/2011/03/07/a-day-in-the-life-of-minecraft-creator-mojang/

Ward, Mark. "Why Minecraft Is More than Just Another Video Game." *BBC News Magazine.* September 6, 2013. http://www.bbc.co.uk/news/magazine-23572742

Books
Cordeiro, Jacob. *Minecraft for Dummies.* Hoboken, NJ: Wiley, 2013.

Goldberg, Daniel, and Linus Larson. *Minecraft: The Unlikely Tale of Markus "Notch" Persson and the Game that Changed Everything.* Translated by Jennifer Hawkins. New York: Seven Stories Press, 2013.

O'Brien, Stephen. *The Ultimate Player's Guide to Minecraft.* Indianapolis: Que Publishing, 2013.

Scholastic, *Minecraft: Essential Handbook: An Official Mojang Book.* New York: Scholastic Books, 2013.

Scholastic, *Minecraft: Redstone Handbook: An Official Mojang Book.* New York: Scholastic Books, 2014.

The NEW (2014) Complete Guide to Minecraft Tricks, Game Cheats, and Guide with Tips and Tricks, Strategy, Walkthrough, Secrets, Codes, Gameplay and More. Amazon Digital Services, 2014.

On the Internet

Minecraft
https://minecraft.net/

MinecraftEdu
http://minecraftedu.com/

Mojang
https://mojang.com/about/

CHAPTER NOTES

Chapter 1

1. Daniel Goldberg and Linus Larson, *Minecraft: The Unlikely Tale of Markus "Notch" Persson and the Game That Changed Everything,* translated by Jennifer Hawkins (New York: Seven Stories Press, 2013), quoted by Eric Johnson, "Book Excerpt: How Minecraft Creator Markus Persson Almost Took a Job at Valve," All Things D, December 9, 2013.
2. Minecraft, Statistics. February 23, 2014.
3. Eddie Makuch, "Minecraft Console Sales Pass PC, Series Nears 54 Million Copies Sold," GameSpot, June 24, 2014.

Chapter 2

1. Simon Parkin, "The Creator," *The New Yorker,* April 5, 2013.
2. Alex Handy, "Interview: Markus 'Notch' Persson Talks Making *Minecraft,*" *Gamasutra*, March 23, 2010.
3. Parkin.
4. Handy.
5. Jamie Russell. "Markus Persson: Interview." BAFTA Guru, March 14, 2012.
6. Ibid.

Chapter 3

1. Simon Parkin, "The Creator," *The New Yorker,* April 5, 2013.
2. Parkin.
3. Jamie Russell, "Markus Persson: Interview," *BAFTA Guru,* March 14, 2012.
4. Parkin.
5. Ibid.
6. Markus Persson, "I Love You, Dad," *The Word of Notch,* December 13, 2012.

Chapter 4

1. Rachel Kolman, "Minecraft Can Now Be Played in School," *WebProNews,* November 17, 2013.
2. Simon Parkin, "The Creator," *The New Yorker,* April 5, 2013.
3. John Walker, "A Day in the Life of Minecraft Creator Mojang," *Rock, Paper, Shotgun,* March 7, 2011.
4. Parkin.

5. "Markus 'Notch' Persson, Mojang CEO, Gives $3 Million to Employees," *Huffington Post,* March 2, 2012.
6. Walker.
7. Tyler Wilde, "Notch Names His Space Game 0x10^c, Says Its Pronunciation Is 'a Riddle,'" *PCGamer,* April 3, 2012.
8. Parkin.

Chapter 5
1. Nick Bilton, "Disruptions: *Minecraft,* an Obsession and an Educational Tool," *The New York Times: Bits,* September 15, 2013.
2. Ibid.
3. John Walker, "A Day in the Life of Minecraft Creator Mojang," *Rock, Paper, Shotgun,* March 7, 2011.
4. Notch on Twitter, December 2, 2011.
5. Kyle Hilliard, "Minecraft's Markus 'Notch' Persson Talks about His Millionaire Status," *Game Informer,* February 2, 2013.
6. Will Freeman, "Interview: The Minecraft Man," *Develop,* October 28, 2010.

GLOSSARY

architect—A person who designs buildings and other large construction projects.

ASCII (ASK-ee)—American Standard Code for Information Interchange—a standard computer code for text and commands that can be read by most electronic devices.

arrogant—Acting excessively prideful.

extravagant—Spending (money) much more than is necessary or wise.

graphic design—The profession of combining images, words, and ideas to convey information to people.

modest—Not showing too much pride.

modification—A slight change.

niche—A place that is just right for a person or thing.

notification—An announcement.

perception—Observation or awareness; way of looking at things.

sandbox game—A type of video game in which a player can roam with very few limitations.

scrutinize—To study closely and thoroughly.

simulation—An imitation made to look, feel, and act like the original.

spaghetti western—Any of the Italian-made movies about the American West.

subsequent—Following or next.